Approaches To How They Behave

W.S. Graham 1918-1986

Sydney Graham was born and brought up in Greenock, and trained as an engineer. In 1943 he settled in Cornwall where the growing colony of experimental artists came to respect the determination and acute self-criticism with which he pursued his work. He suffered severe poverty without self-pity. Artists Sven Berlin, Terry Frost, Roger Hilton, Peter Lanyon, Ben Nicholson, Michael Seward Snow, Karl Weschke and Bryan Wynter were among many friends who shared their landscape with him. Some of them had known the old St Ives fisherman Alfred Wallis whose lively 'naïve' paintings became seen as a necessary counterbalance to the moribund academic tradition. Graham himself frequently used the images and speech of his Scottish childhood in his work. All his poetry was to demonstrate an awareness of the materials of his craft – words, sound, rhythm, clarity of speech and a healthy Scottish directness of address. In 1949 T.S. Eliot adopted his work and Faber and Faber published all his subsequent poetry. Since his death, the importance of Graham's achievement has been widely acknowledged. Key posthumous works are *New Collected Poems* (Faber and Faber, 2004) and *The Nightfisherman – Selected Letters of W.S. Graham* (Carcanet Press, 1999).

Approaches To How They Behave

W.S. Graham

Donut Press

Published by Donut Press in March 2009.

Donut Press, PO Box 45093,
London, N4 1UZ.
www.donutpress.co.uk

Printed and bound by
The Colourhouse,
Arklow Road Trading Estate, Arklow Road,
London, SE14 6EB.

ISBN: 9780955360435

A CIP record for this book is available
from the British Library.

Contents

W.S. Graham 1918-1986, ii
Acknowledgements, vi
The Music of Anxiety, by Sean O'Brien, vii
Approaches To How They Behave, 3
Author photograph, 19
Graham on Graham, 20

Acknowledgements

'Approaches To How They Behave' first appeared in
Malcolm Mooney's Land (Faber and Faber, 1970) and is also
included in *Selected Poems* (Faber and Faber, 1996) and
New Collected Poems (Faber & Faber, 2004).

Extracts from W.S. Graham's correspondence are taken
from *The Nightfisherman – Selected Letters of W.S. Graham*
(Carcanet, 1999).

Author photograph © Michael Seward Snow, 2009

Donut Press would like to thank Michael and Margaret
Snow for their contribution to this publication. We also
thank them, as executors of the Estate of W.S. Graham, for
their permission to reproduce the above mentioned material.
Thanks are also sent to Sean O'Brien.

Requests for W.S Graham copyright permissions should
be addressed to Michael and Mararet Snow, Stonemark,
Hillerton Cross, Spreyton, Devon, EX17 5AS.

The Music of Anxiety

'(Christ the words Edwin so difficult and so unspeaking when you want them to help)'

W.S. Graham, letter to Edwin Morgan, 22nd September 1943

Since the publication of *New Collected Poems* (2004), the poetry of W.S. Graham may have moved from being something of a secret to the stage where he is read with interest but not always with confidence. Critics including Tony Lopez and Matthew Francis have done much to elucidate Graham's poems; yet to new readers the strangeness of his work may make it seem like a report from a world adjacent but by no means identical to this one, somewhere dismayingly abstract to those accustomed to the physical realism of Seamus Heaney or Ted Hughes.

Moreover, the address from which Graham writes is one where the unexamined common sense which still sustains much of our thinking is put to the test by the very instrument which normally affirms it – language – and found wanting. The ground is taken from under us. It seems that 'this' world, the everyday taken-for-granted one, is a fiction: everyday pragmatism about our power to communicate is based on a convenient metaphor, and is more of an aspiration or jury-rigged operating necessity than it is a fact.

Although he was interested in philosophy, Graham's handling of his material is urgent and far from academic, and perhaps its special challenge lies in what might be called the intimidating simplicity it offers, in passages of wit, comedy, great beauty and profound feeling – poetry with the blinkers and bandages removed, offering the music of an intense anxiety and love. Graham had no other *modus vivendi* than to struggle with language.

When T.S. Eliot, no mean judge, took on Graham's work for Faber, he warned him that its complexity might mean that the poems 'went slowly' with the audience. Graham himself contributed to this snail's pace. A poet of repute in the 1940s, he virtually vanished after *The Nightfishing* (1955). Not until *Malcolm Mooney's Land* (1970) did his poetry re-emerge, somewhat changed, barer, starker, interiorized. It is from this book that the fifteen-part 'Approaches To How They Behave' is drawn – from what might be called 'early later' Graham – and the poem offers a very clear declaration of his concerns. 'They', of course, are words.

Of the words he uses, the poet declares in the opening section: 'I would like to see where they go / And how without me they behave.' This is to ask the impossible: for example one person cannot know directly how another experiences a poem. Into this apparent bareness Graham introduces a note of combined wistfulness and mischief. Following the opening iamb with two anapaests, that last line evokes the notion of language being 'entertained and charmed' elsewhere by moving into a dance step. This little 'canter' then lends force by contrast to the plainness with which the second section opens ('Speaking is difficult', though of course Graham is writing, not speaking, writing having to stand in for the presumed directness of speech) and makes room for a formulation which is, typically, both plain and strange: 'one tries / To be exact and yet not to / Exact the prime intention to death.'

If this recalls anybody, it's Shakespeare, in its swift, bare, multifoliate suggestiveness (compare the Duke advising Claudio in *Measure for Measure*: 'Be absolute for death'). The actual Shakespearean reference here might be to *The Merchant of Venice* and Shylock's insistence on the literal 'exaction' of the pound of flesh. 'One' must avoid killing language by closing down its possibilities (not that in fact one could ...); the insistence on the literal meaning, 'the letter', is deathly in the sense indicated in 2 Corinthians 3.6: 'The letter killeth, but the spirit giveth life.' Graham's rhetoric, with its recurrent slight strangeness, draws powerfully on the memory of scripture. For example, the immediately preceding verse from 2 Corinthians would not be out of place here: 'Not that we are sufficient of ourselves to think any thing as of ourselves ...'

The Shakespearean analogy resurfaces in section 5, when the words talk to each other. Servants of 'a doubtful god', their philosophical, half-amused grumbling recalls the soldiers in *Henry V*. For a poetry of isolation, Graham's work is extremely sociable and comic. Equally, for a 'poetry of ideas' it is conspicuously dramatic in its nagging ruminations. Trying to read Graham's poems as linear examinations of their material is unsatisfactory: the reader's attention will find itself shrugged off by the poems – see sections 6, 7 and 8. The 'ideas' about language and the mysterious inaccessibility of the other person, the reader or listener, come to life as drama, as performance, in the sense of the poem as an event rather than a memorial, in the continuous re-addressing of abiding anxieties. These reveries might well care to be more coolly analytical but they are continually interrupted and redirected by past, future, chance and the edge of the present moment. In one sense the logic under which the poems move forward is musical, a matter of motifs, responses, recapitulations and reformulations – a logic of form. Yet the speaker is also always beginning again, as at the close of the poem, in 'A new silence I hope to break' – though consciousness cannot step outside itself and come in by another door.

The other playwright with whom Graham invites comparison is, of course, Beckett, whose response to limits – of understanding, of freedom – is likewise an exacting music. It was by means of such music that Graham claimed the margin of paradoxical freedom that enabled him to act on an early declaration to his friend Edwin Morgan: 'The poet does not write what he knows but what he doesn't know', words which in turn connect him as clearly to the imaginative enthusiasm of Keats as to the scepticism of twentieth century philosophy. Graham's poetry is the opposite of Parnassian: it is a poetry of urgent excitement, bracing and invigorating as a drenching with icy water.

Sean O'Brien,
Newcastle, January 2009.

Approaches To How They Behave

W.S. Graham

1

What does it matter if the words
I choose, in the order I choose them in,
Go out into a silence I know
Nothing about, there to be let
In and entertained and charmed
Out of their master's orders? And yet
I would like to see where they go
And how without me they behave.

2

Speaking is difficult and one tries
To be exact and yet not to
Exact the prime intention to death.
On the other hand the appearance of things
Must not be made to mean another
Thing. It is a kind of triumph
To see them and to put them down
As what they are. The inadequacy
Of the living, animal language drives
Us all to metaphor and an attempt
To organize the spaces we think
We have made occur between the words.

3

The bad word and the bad word and
The word which glamours me with some
Quick face it pulls to make me let
It leave me to go across
In roughly your direction, hates
To go out maybe so completely
On another silence not its own.

4

Before I know it they are out
Afloat in the head which freezes them.
Then I suppose I take the best
Away and leave the others arranged
Like floating bergs to sink a convoy.

5

One word says to its mate O
I do not think we go together
Are we doing any good here
Why do we find ourselves put down?
The mate pleased to be spoken to
Looks up from the line below
And says well that doubtful god
Who has us here is far from sure
How we on our own tickle the chin
Of the prince or the dame that lets us in.

6

The dark companion is a star
Very present like a dark poem
Far and unreadable just out
At the edge of this poem floating.
It is not more or less a dark
Companion poem to the poem.

7

Language is expensive if
We want to strut, busked out
Showing our best on silence.
Good Morning. That is a bonny doing
Of verbs you wear with the celandine
Catching the same sun as mine.
You wear your dress like a prince but
A country's prince beyond my ken.
Through the chinks in your lyric coat
My ear catches a royal glimpse
Of fuzzed flesh, unworded body.
Was there something you wanted to say?
I myself dress up in what I can
Afford on the broadway. Underneath
My overcoat of the time's slang
I am fashionable enough wearing
The grave-clothes of my generous masters.

8

And what are you supposed to say
I asked a new word but it kept mum.
I had secretly admired always
What I thought it was here for.
But I was wrong when I looked it up
Between the painted boards. It said
Something it was never very likely
I could fit in to a poem in my life.

9

The good word said I am not pressed
For time. I have all the foxglove day
And all my user's days to give
You my attention. Shines the red
Fox in the digitalis grove.
Choose me choose me. Guess which
Word I am here calling myself
The best. If you can't fit me in
To lying down here among the fox
Glove towers of the moment, say
I am yours the more you use me. Tomorrow
Same place same time give me a ring.

10

Backwards the poem's just as good.
We human angels as we read
Read back as we gobble the words up.
Allowing the poem to represent
A recognizable landscape
Sprouting green up or letting green
With all its weight of love hang
To gravity's sweet affection,
Arse-versa it is the same object,
Even although the last word seems
To have sung first, or the breakfast lark
Sings up from the bottom of the sea.

11

The poem is not a string of knots
Tied for a meaning of another time
And country, unreadable, found
By chance. The poem is not a henge
Or Easter Island emerged Longnose
Or a tally used by early unknown
Peoples. The words we breathe and puff
Are our utensils down the dream
Into the manhole. Replace the cover.

12

The words are mine. The thoughts are all
Yours as they occur behind
The bat of your vast unseen eyes.
These words are as you see them put
Down on the dead-still page. They have
No ability above their station.
Their station on silence is exact.
What you do with them is nobody's business.

13

Running across the language lightly
This morning in the hangingover
Whistling light from the window, I
Was tripped and caught into the whole
Formal scheme which Art is.
I had only meant to enjoy
Dallying between the imaginary
And imaginary's opposite
With a thought or two up my sleeve.

14

Is the word? Yes Yes. But I hear
A sound without words from another
Person I can't see at my elbow.
A sigh to be proud of. You? Me?

15

Having to construct the silence first
To speak out on I realize
The silence even itself floats
At my ear-side with a character
I have not met before. Hello
Hello I shout but that silence
Floats steady, will not be marked
By an off-hand shout. For some reason
It refuses to be broken now
By what I thought was worth saying.
If I wait a while, if I look out
At the heavy greedy rooks on the wall
It will disperse. Now I construct
A new silence I hope to break.

W.S. Graham, circa 1958.

Graham on Graham

To Ruth Hilton

The thing is to find or create (in this case the same thing)
a language, a timbre of thought or voice, which I will live in.
It will never be adequate except for its moment but it will be
the nearest to my soul speaking and as I change so it shall.
A way of speaking, if it is any good, as it persists creates its
understanders. Its early idiosyncracies become solid currency.
It is alive, changing and organic. And at last works. (1967)

To Edwin Morgan

I have been seeing Eliot quite a lot ...We have talked mostly
about verse and what he remarked about my own was
cheering ... [H]e said that I had 'a good sense of form and a
wonderful sense of rhythm.' He suggested that my poetry was
'intellectual' poetry and would go slow because people just
were lazy about thinking. (1949)

I have been shaken up in the last three years by my study of
Pound and Eliot ... [T]he way they have used different textures of
thought and idiom in the same poem (like montage) is new, an
addition, a widening of the possibilities of what a poet may say ...
I want to write 'harder', the poems having more shape, being more
abstract, the verse not so brow-beaten still by the Shakespearean
iambic line. And yet I want my poems to be more than ever a valid
extension of the possibilities of the language. (1950)

To Robin Skelton

What a mysterious, unsubstantial business it is, writing poetry. After one finishes a poem which seems to work one says Ha Ha now I'll write another because I know how to do it but it is not so. There is the silence before one just as difficult to disturb significantly as before. What one has learned is inadequate against the new silence presented. (1972)

To Roger Hilton

I wish you didn't think those last poems were too obscure. I thought I was making some headway in uniting you with another medium viz poetry. You can't have it completely understood in that way all the time. Allow yourself to encounter the mystery occasionally and don't ask the thing from an object which it is not. (1965)

I mean no harm, I say. But of course I mean every harm by speaking with a degree of articulateness above the average about the things which disturb us all I hope. (1969)

I am pleased you are trying my poetry. What it says I think you would believe in. Take it easy. As well you know it is not meant to be 'above' you. It is meant to be above me. Of course there are good lines. By this time I am expert enough to be able to make good lines. I hope I am better than that and move the heart. (1970)